Sunflowers and Silence:

Reflections from the Valley

*A Memoir and Guided Journal Through
Grief, Boundaries, and Healing*

Misty Reshun

CONTENTS

- The Call That Changed Everything

- A Letter to Myself in That Moment

- When I Didn't Know What to Do

- When I Ask God, "Why Would You Allow This?"

- A Letter to God

- Be Specific With Your Prayers

- The Last Message

- His Name was Derrion

- The Silence Without Goodbye

Part IV: Boundaries, Forgiveness & Becoming - 95

Part V: Life With MiMi - 114

Part VI: Legacy Letters - 131

Part VII: What Remains - 145

DEDICATION

For my sons, Derrion, whose life and loss changed mine forever, and Cameron, who reminds me every day that love continues.

For my grandchildren, Dezmon, Derrion Jr., Suede, and Za'Niyah, who call me MiMi and give me reasons to smile through the ache.

For every parent who has loved in silence, hoped in pain, and chosen healing one breath at a time, this is for you.

Introduction

This is not the book I ever thought I'd write.

I dreamed of writing something joyful, maybe even lighthearted, stories about family, travel, or hard-won wisdom from the twists and turns of life. But this? A memoir born out of heartbreak and healing? A guided journal for parents navigating pain? I didn't see it coming.

But loss changes everything.

When my son Derrion died, I found myself unraveling in ways I didn't know were possible. The grief wasn't just about his absence, it was layered, tangled in the history we shared, the distance we endured, and the heartbreak of everything that went unsaid. I wasn't just mourning a child. I was mourning what we never got to fix. The mother I used to be. The future I once hoped for.

In the stillness that followed the storm, I began to write. Not to make sense of the loss, not at first, but to survive it. To breathe through it. To speak what silence tried to steal from me. And what poured out wasn't just my story. It was a conversation with God, with grief, with myself, and with other parents who carry invisible weight.

You'll find those conversations here.

Some pages read like a journal. Others like a prayer. Some are letters I never got to send. Others are truths I didn't know I was allowed to say out loud. But all of it is real. All of it is mine. And if even one word speaks to your story too, then this offering has done its work.

Let me be clear: This book holds faith, but it also holds questions. I talk to God in these pages, but I also talk back. Whether you share my faith, follow another path, or hold no beliefs at all, I hope you'll find space here to breathe, reflect, and feel seen. You don't need to be in a church to belong to a story of healing. You just need a heart that's still beating.

There's one more truth I want to name before we begin. Derrion's father, Brian Robinson, is not the focus of this book, but he is part of our story. They were close for many years. Addiction, on both sides, hurt them both. And while I won't dwell on his part of the journey, that story is not mine to tell, I want to honor that early bond because it mattered. Because love always matters.

And as I share the truth of our story, there is one more boundary I hold gently but firmly:
Out of love and privacy, I still choose to protect my son. Some details will remain sacred. His dignity matters too much to me to offer up his pain for public consumption. This book is not about blame. It's about honesty, healing, and humanity.
So here we are.
In the valley. Among sunflowers. In the space where silence can finally speak.

If you've ever struggled to love someone who was hurting you...
If you've ever set a boundary that broke your heart...

If you've lost a child or a relationship or a dream...

If you are navigating grief in any form...

This is for you.

Take what you need. Skip what you don't. Come back as many times as you want.

You are not alone.

Reader's Note: About the Faith Reflections

Throughout this book, you'll see moments where I speak directly to God. Some pages are full of faith. Others are full of questions. Many hold both.

The heart behind these reflections is not doctrine.

It's truth.

Truth wrapped in pain. Truth rooted in love. Truth whispered in the silence.

If a prayer resonates, receive it.

If it doesn't, reinterpret it through your own lens.

This is not about religion. It's about humanity.

Whether you believe in God, honor your ancestors, connect to nature, the universe, or something else entirely, you are welcome here. Grief does not discriminate. Neither does healing.

Take what speaks to you. Leave what doesn't.

This is your space too.

On Protecting His Dignity

There is something instinctive, almost primal, about a parent's desire to protect their child. That impulse does not disappear with age, distance, conflict, or even death. Whether our children are thriving or troubled, close to us or estranged, our hearts still reach to shield them—from judgment, from harm, from the harshness of a world that may never fully understand who they are, were or what they carried.

That is why I'm writing this carefully. Not to expose Derrion's pain, but to honor his humanity.

I wrote this to remember my son, not to relive his worst moments. I wrote it to honor the complexity of being his mother. Of grieving a child you loved deeply and struggled with just as deeply. I know I'm not the only one holding both.

There are things I will never share in this book. Things I won't publish or unpack. I've done that privately and through therapy. Not because they don't matter, but because they belong to him. Because protecting his dignity, even in death, is my last act of love.

The world doesn't need another tragedy to dissect. What we need is tenderness. Truth-telling that doesn't come at the cost of someone's soul.

So let this be clear: Derrion was more than his struggles. He was brilliant. Funny. Protective. Tender-hearted. He had a smile that lit up a room and a laugh that stayed with you. He loved deeply, even when he didn't know how to show it. He was a father, a son, and a writer. He authored *The Love Boyz* and left behind an unpublished work titled *Christian's Pain*.

He was trying—sometimes in silence, sometimes in chaos, always in his own way. And I believe he knew I loved him, even when my boundaries looked like distance and lack of care.

I carry all of that with me.

If you're a parent grieving a complicated loss, please know this: You don't owe the world your child's lowest moments. You can tell your truth and still protect theirs. That is not secrecy.

That is sacred.

That is love.

Preface: Why Sunflowers?

I was already in the valley.

Long before grief came crashing in, I had been walking through shadows, parenting in hard places, holding hope in one hand and heartbreak in the other. Addiction. Estrangement. The quiet ache of watching someone you love drift in and out of reach. That valley was already mine.

Then, one day, I was buried even deeper.
My son, Derrion, was gone, and with him went the version of motherhood I had imagined, fought for, and held onto, even in the hardest seasons. The silence grew heavier. The soil, thicker. And yet, even there, something stirred. Not all at once. Not every day. But little by little, hope started pressing its way toward the surface.

That's when I started thinking about sunflowers, my favorite flower since I was a girl.
Sunflowers turn toward the sun even on the darkest days, a powerful metaphor for resilience and hope. They grow tall and strong, but only after beginning as small seeds buried in the dirt, just like us in our grief.

And even as the world turns, they follow the light, always reaching for warmth and life.

They bloom in the valley.
They rise anyway.

This book is for anyone who's ever been planted in pain and is still learning how to grow. It's for the mothers, the fathers, the grandparents, the loved ones who've stood in silence, stared at the ceiling, begged for a second chance, or tried to love someone through addiction, estrangement, or loss.

These reflections are pieces of my journey. They are raw, honest, and still in progress because healing isn't a straight path. Some days, I'm the seed. Some days I'm the bloom. Most days, I'm both.
And then there's the silence.

Grief doesn't always speak in words. Sometimes, it settles into the stillness, into the long pauses, the unanswered questions, the prayers we can't quite say out loud. I've come to understand that silence isn't empty. It holds truth. Memory. Love. And sometimes, the deepest

healing happens when nothing is spoken at all.

This book honors that silence.

The silence between mother and son.

The silence between heartache and hope.

The silence of loss, and the quiet strength it takes to keep going.

Wherever you are in your own valley, may you find your way toward the light.

We don't have to bloom perfectly.

We just have to bloom.

ACKNOWLEDGMENTS

To my family and closest friends, thank you for walking beside me through the shadows and the light. Your love is the thread that holds me together, even in the hardest chapters. Yolanda, Sherrie, and the one who shared that season of life with me — thank you for never leaving my side when I needed it most. Your presence carried me through.

To my ex-husband, Keith Irby — thank you for always being my rock and for encouraging me to write long before I ever believed I could. I never imagined that tragedy would be the catalyst, but your steady presence and unwavering belief in me laid the foundation. Even when our paths shifted, your support remained, and it has meant more than words can express. I see now that you always believed in me.

To The Regal Sisterhood Book Club, thank you for nearly two decades of laughter, sisterhood, and stories that shaped my soul. You've given me space to speak, grieve, grow, and remember who I am.

To my therapist, Takeisha Watson, thank you for creating a space where I could fall apart and rebuild, piece by piece. Your guidance has been a sacred part of this journey.

And to every parent, grandparent, child, sibling, or grieving soul who finds themselves in these pages, thank you for showing up. Your story matters. You are not alone.

Part I: When Goodbye Became Silent

"Some storms don't give warnings. They just arrive and change everything."
—Misty Reshun

Sometimes, goodbye doesn't come with closure — only silence. A shift in the soul. A quiet unraveling that says everything has changed, even if no one's found the words yet. This section captures those moments — where love reached, fear lingered, and the goodbye became silent long before I was ready to let go.

- Included Titles:

  - The Call That Changed Everything

  - A Letter to Myself in That Moment

  - When I Didn't Know What to Do

  - When I Ask God, "Why Would You Allow This?"

  - A Letter to God

  - Be Specific With Your Prayers

  - Reflection: The Last Message

  - His Name was Derrion

  - The Silence Without Goodbye

The Call That Changed Everything

It was a moment that split my life into before and after.

I got the call from my mother. I could hear panic in her voice. She didn't say much, just that Derrion's friend needed to speak with me. When she handed him the phone, my mind immediately jumped to the familiar pattern: He must have been arrested again.

That thought didn't come from judgment. It came from experience. From the many times I had gotten calls like that before. The rollercoaster of loving someone who struggles and holding your breath every time the phone rings.

But this call was different.

Nothing could have prepared me for what his friend actually said.

They had gone to the lake. There had been some kind of event. And Derrion... drowned.

Drowned.

The word didn't register at first. My brain couldn't make sense of it. My heart refused to believe it. I was waiting for a correction, for him to say, "But he's okay," or "They pulled him out in time."

But that correction never came.

I don't remember what else was said. I don't even remember the young man's name. Everything after that became a blur, sounds, colors, time, suspended in grief.

In that moment, my life stopped.

My son was gone.

And so was the version of me that existed before that call.

It's hard to explain how quickly a single phone call can gut you.

How everything you knew, or thought you knew, unravels in an instant.

I lost my first born son.

And I lost a part of myself, too.

Journal Prompt:

Reflect on the moment you first received devastating news, whether it was the loss of a child, a diagnosis, or a fracture in a relationship. What were the first words that left your lips? What emotions rose to the surface? What did you need most in that moment, and did anyone provide it?

Write without judgment. Let your heart speak freely.

You might begin with:

- The moment I heard the words, I...

- What I thought I was about to hear was...

- I still carry the weight of that call because...

- My body remembers...

- If I could speak to myself in that moment now, I would say...

_____

_____

_____

_____

_____

Affirmation
Even in the blur of pain, I survived that moment.
I am still standing. I honor my heart for carrying me through the unthinkable.

A Letter to Myself in That Moment

Dear Me,

I know you're in shock right now.

You're holding the phone, but it feels like your whole world is slipping through your fingers. You just heard something you cannot believe, something you were never prepared to hear. You are trying to make sense of the words, but they don't make sense. You want to scream, run, collapse... but all you can do is stand there, stunned.

I see you.

 I see the moment your heart cracked open. I see the silence behind your eyes. I see how the world faded into a blur around you. You are not weak. You are in grief. You are in trauma. And still, somehow, you are surviving the moment that was meant to destroy you.

You won't remember the name of the person who gave you the tragic news. You won't remember what you were doing before the phone rang. But you will remember that moment, the one that changed everything.

And you will live through it.

You will carry pain so deep, no one will fully understand it. But you will also carry love just as deep. Love for Derrion. Love for your other son, Cameron. Love for the version of you who is learning how to breathe again, one fragile breath at a time.

You won't have all the answers. You're not supposed to. But you will keep going. And every step you take is a step of courage.

So when you feel like you can't do this, remember:
You already are.

With all my love,

Me

When I Didn't Know What to Do

"God, why would You allow this?"

"I don't know what to do."

Those were the only words I could manage the day I found out my son, Derrion, had died.

I whispered them. I shouted them. I wept them into the silence of a world that had just turned upside down. The pain was so heavy, I could barely breathe. I wasn't just a mother grieving, I was a mother shattered.

I had always believed it was my job to protect him, guide him, help him through.

And in that moment, I felt like I had failed.

I know now that I didn't fail, I loved.

And love doesn't die with the person.

It just aches in a new way.

People often think faith is about having answers.

But I've learned that real faith is what rises when nothing makes sense.

It's crying out to God with your whole heart, even when you're met with silence.

It's getting up the next day, even if your legs shake.

It's loving your grandchildren when your own child is gone.

It's holding space for the ache, while still honoring the memory.

If you've ever been there, grieving, lost, not knowing what to do, please hear this:

You are not weak.

You are not broken.

You are human. You are grieving.

You are not alone.

I still don't have all the answers.

But I have love.

I have memories.

And I have a voice.

Today, I use it to honor my son.

Journal Prompt:

Think back to a time when you truly did not know what to do.

What did that moment feel like in your body? In your spirit?

Were you angry, numb, panicked, or all three?

What words, prayers, or cries rose up in you, and how were they received by those around you—or by God?

What do you wish someone had said or done for you in that moment?

How do you see that version of yourself now?

You might begin with:

- I couldn't move because...
- I prayed, but...
- In that moment, what I needed most was...
- I no longer judge myself for...
- My faith looked like...

_____

_____

_____

_____

Affirmation:
Even when I don't know what to do, I can still breathe, still feel, still love. I am allowed to grieve, and I am worthy of healing.

When I Asked God, *"Why Would You Allow This?"*

After the call.

After the words I never expected to hear.

After my world shattered in a single breath,

I went straight to God.

And I didn't whisper a gentle prayer.

I didn't quote scripture or ask for peace.

I cried out from a place so raw, it didn't feel like prayer at all.

It felt like pleading.

Accusing.

Collapsing.

"God, why would You allow this?"

I wasn't asking for a sermon.

I wasn't trying to understand some divine plan.

I just wanted to know why.

Why my son?

Why now?

Why like this?

And when no answer came, I kept repeating the only thing I could say:

"I don't know what to do. I don't know what to do. I don't know what to do."

It was all I had left.

My soul didn't know how to do anything else but weep and question.

There's a kind of grief that strips you bare.

It peels away every layer of who you thought you were and leaves you face-to-face with your own broken heart.

That's where I was.

That's what I offered God.

Not strength.

Not faith.

Just truth.

And somehow, even in the silence, I believe God heard me.

I believe my tears were prayers.

My questions were sacred.

My confusion was allowed.

Journal Prompt:

Think back to your first raw, honest thoughts after your loss. Who or what did you turn to? Was it God? The universe? Your ancestors? Your inner knowing? Or did you feel completely alone? Use this space to write about the questions you had, the emotions you released, and the weight of what you were holding. This is a space for your truth—whatever it looks like.

You might begin with:

- My first words were...

- I couldn't believe that...

- What I still don't understand is...

- I didn't know who to turn to, but I...

- What I needed in that moment was...

_____

_____

_____

_____

_____

Affirmation:
God can handle my anger, my sorrow, and my questions.
Even when I don't understand, I am still held.

A Letter to God

Dear God,

I don't even know where to begin.

When Derrion died, I came to You broken. I came to You sobbing, screaming, confused.

I asked You why You would allow this.

I told You, over and over again, I don't know what to do.

I was clinging to You, not because I was strong, but because I was desperate.

But then something else happened.

A few days later, my mother, grieving too, I know, said something that cut me even deeper.

When I asked her again, Why would God allow this?, she said:

"God wants us to obey Him."

In that moment, I didn't just feel grief, I felt shame.

It felt like she was saying this was my fault.

That because I made a decision she didn't agree with, because I left a marriage that no longer held life for me, You were now punishing me by taking my son.

And God... I just don't believe that's who you are.

I've tried to wrap my heart around it.

Tried to understand how someone could think that way.

Tried to make peace with the idea that maybe You are still good, even when the people who claim to speak for You say harmful things.

But I need to say this:

That hurt me deeply.

It confused my spirit.

It made me question Your love.

And I'm still trying to heal from the double wound of loss and blame.

So, I'm asking You again, from a quieter place now:

Are You really a Father who takes a child from a parent to teach a lesson?

Is obedience what You care about more than my heart?

Can You hold my pain, even when it's messy and filled with anger?

I'm still here, God.

Still broken.

Still asking.

Still hoping You are who I want to believe You are.

And maybe that's faith.

Or maybe it's just love.

Either way... I'm still talking to You.

And I need You to still be listening.

Love,

Your daughter

Journal Prompt:

Have you ever received words from someone close to you that added pain to your grief instead of easing it? What was said, and how did it make you feel?

Take time to unpack the moment, what it stirred in you, what you wish had been said instead, and how your faith or relationship with God was impacted as a result.

You might begin with:
- When she said..., I felt...
- What I really needed to hear in that moment was...
- That experience made me question...
- I'm still trying to reconcile...

_____

_____

_____

_____

_____

Affirmation:

God is a loving parent who welcomes my pain, my questions, and my need for comfort.
Even when my choices don't align with others' expectations, God remains merciful and near.
I may not have all the answers, but I am still held in love.
My grief is not a punishment, and my heart is safe with God.

Be Specific With Your Prayers

I remember saying to Derrion on several occasions, "I pray you're not doing the same things when you're 40." It was my way of holding on to hope, of believing he would outgrow the cycle, change, choose life in a different way.

I guess my prayer was answered.
He passed just days shy of his 37th birthday.

I never imagined him not being here to see 40 would be how that prayer was fulfilled. I didn't mean it like that. I didn't mean this.

Now I sit with the question: was that protection? Divine intervention? Mercy? Or just the cold hand of fate?

Sometimes our prayers are answered in ways we never intended, and the outcomes leave us with more questions than peace. I still talk to God about it. I still ask why.

And I still pray. But now, I pray differently. With more clarity. With trembling hope. And with the hard-earned wisdom that even a mother's prayers don't come with guarantees.

Journal Prompt:

What is a prayer you once prayed for a loved one that was answered differently than you expected? How do you reconcile that answer with your faith, your grief, or your understanding of divine intention?

_____

_____

_____

_____

_____

Affirmation:

Even when I didn't understand the outcome, my prayers were rooted in love. I trust that love still echoes beyond what I can see.

The Last Message

In the days after Derrion passed, I found myself going through his cell phone. I don't know what I was searching for exactly. Maybe a trace of peace. Maybe answers. Maybe just something that still felt like him.

That's when I saw the texts.

Just a day or so before he died, he had sent out several messages to various friends with the same link—a YouTube video of DMX's song *"I'm Ready to Meet Him."* Over and over, that title stared back at me, cutting through the noise of my grief like a whisper wrapped in thunder. He was reaching out with something bigger than words. That song wasn't random. It was deliberate. It was Derrion speaking with the voice of someone who knew he was standing on the edge.

He was facing another long jail sentence. Another stretch of time stolen by the system, the struggle, the cycle. And I know, in my heart, the last thing he wanted was to go back behind those walls. Maybe the thought of going back broke something in him that was already hanging by a thread.

But that song... that song felt like a surrender. Not in weakness, but in weariness. In honesty. In spirit. It told me he was making peace, in the only way he could. He was talking to God in his own voice. In his own way.

When it came time to write his obituary, I knew I had to include it. I took words from that song and shaped them into a letter—a simulated message from him to the world. Because even if he didn't say goodbye with his voice, he left us with something that sounded a lot like farewell.

That discovery hurt. But it also helped. It let me believe that maybe, just maybe, he had made some kind of peace before he left. And that he wasn't alone when he crossed over—he was heard.

Journal Prompt:

What signs or messages, expected or unexpected, have offered you peace in the midst of your grief? How do you interpret them now, with time and reflection?

_____

_____

_____

_____

_____

Affirmation:

Even in the silence, I am being spoken to. I trust that peace can arrive in forms I don't always understand.

His Name Was Derrion

I will always protect my son's dignity, even in death.

He struggled with addiction. He was in pain. And he made choices that broke my heart and fractured our family.

But he was still mine.

He was brilliant, funny, protective, and tender-hearted. He had a smile that lit up a room and a laugh that stayed with you. He loved deeply, even when he didn't know how to show it.

His name was Derrion Dante' Robinson, but I called him Derry Don. He was highly intelligent, a gifted thinker, and a writer. He authored *The Love Boyz* and was working on another novel, *Christian's Pain,* that has yet to be published. He loved football and had a natural talent for chess, a game that matched his strategic mind.

I'm learning how to be honest about what happened, without shame, without sugarcoating, and without putting his memory on trial.

That balance? It's delicate. But it's necessary.

I can grieve my child while also grieving what never got healed between us.

This journey I'm on—writing, remembering, reckoning—it's all part of my healing.

And if you've lost a child or are estranged from one... I want you to know: it's okay to talk about the complexity.

You don't owe anyone a neat, tidy version of your pain. You just owe yourself the chance to heal.

I've made a choice to write honestly. Not out of bitterness. Not for attention.

But because silence can feel like shame... I'm choosing healing instead.

So I will share, with care.

I will protect his dignity while honoring my truth.

And I will hold space for other parents navigating the same pain.

Journal Prompt:

Have you ever felt pressure to sanitize or defend your child's story after their death or estrangement? What parts of their truth have you struggled to share out loud, and why?
How do you balance honoring their memory with acknowledging the pain they may have caused?

You might begin with:
- People think my child was... but what they don't know is...
- What I wish I could say without judgment is...
- I feel protective of their memory because...
- I want to speak the truth about my child, but...
- I'm learning that healing looks like...

_____

_____

_____

_____

_____

Affirmation:

I can honor my child's full story without shame or apology.
Grief is not meant to be edited, and neither is love.
I protect their dignity by telling the truth—with compassion, with courage, and with care.

The Silence Without Goodbye

I've known loss before — grandparents, relatives, people I loved. I've even known estrangement. I've lived through heartbreak, disappointment, and the ache of people walking away. But nothing — *nothing* — prepared me for this.

The silence after my son's death is unlike anything I've ever known. Not the kind of silence that brings peace, but the kind that haunts. A silence that holds all the things I didn't get to say. A silence that roars with every missed chance. We hadn't spoken in over a year. We were still fractured. And now, we are frozen.

There was no final conversation. No closure.
No goodbye.

People ask how I'm doing. And all I can say is — *the finality is too much to bear.*

It's not just that he's gone. It's that every version of healing we could've reached together is now sealed in the past.

Every word I hoped to say. Every hug I thought I'd still have time for.

Gone.

I've never lost a spouse. I've never buried a partner.

But this — losing someone who came from my body, who shared my blood, my breath, my name,

This is a grief that redefines what silence sounds like.

And in that silence — the silence without goodbye — I am learning how to live again.

Not by moving on, but by carrying forward.

Not by forgetting, but by *remembering well*.

Journal Prompt:
How do you process grief when there was no goodbye?
What would you say now if given the chance — to them, to yourself, or to God?

_____

_____

_____

_____

_____

Affirmation:
Even without goodbye, my love remains.
I am allowed to grieve the silence, mourn the missed repair, and still carry a legacy of love.

Part II: The Weight of the Pew

"Grief doesn't start with the funeral. Sometimes it begins long before the goodbye."
—Misty Reshun

Faith has always been part of my story, but grief makes even the strongest beliefs feel fragile. Here, I wrestle with the heaviness of sitting in pews while carrying questions that sermons don't always answer. It's about searching for God in the silence, and learning to pray with a heart that's been cracked open.

- Included Titles:
  - I'm Sorry
  - The Front Pew
  - The Unspoken Grief
  - Misunderstood, But Still Mine
  - Eternal Peace
  - Sunflower Goodbye
  - Prayer/Transition: A Prayer in the In-Between
  - Two Sons, One Loss
  - A Letter to Cameron

"I'm Sorry"

The day I viewed Derrion's body, before the funeral, is burned into my memory with searing clarity. Surrounded by family, I walked into that quiet room and saw him—my son—laid out in a beautiful suit, every detail immaculate. He looked so handsome. So still. So final.

The moment my eyes landed on him, my heart screamed louder than my voice could manage. "I'm sorry," I cried out, the words bursting from somewhere deeper than I knew existed. It wasn't an apology of regret for holding a boundary—it was sorrow for the need of that boundary in the first place. For the pain and chaos that made it necessary. For the way our final days were marked not by peace, but by painful space.

What followed next is something I will never forget.

"That's why people shouldn't hold grudges," my sister said, her words sharp, loud, and unrelenting—slicing through the silence like a blade.

She didn't understand. Maybe she didn't want to. Or maybe it was easier to believe the version of the story that came from him.

Because the truth is—I had told her. I had called my mother and both of my sisters immediately after that last encounter with Derrion. I was still crying, shaking, still trembling from the confrontation that had felt both violent and surreal. I recounted everything in real time, my voice thick with fear, heartbreak, and disbelief.

But Derrion told a different story. One crafted by a mind distorted by addiction and narcissism. And she believed him. She decided I had overreacted. That I'd exaggerated. Lied, even. As if I could make up something that had nearly broken me in two. As if a mother would fabricate pain like that for attention or sympathy.

No—I hadn't lied. I hadn't exaggerated. I had survived. I had protected myself. And truthfully, I had tried to protect him too.

Maybe he didn't mean to push me. Maybe in his mind, he didn't see it the way I did. Maybe he shared what he felt rather than what actually happened.

Maybe his version was shaped by his intent, not by the impact. But the fact remains—he did push me. He crossed a line that changed everything.

And I don't tell this story out of spite. I tell it because it's part of the truth. A heartbreaking, complicated truth. The kind that doesn't have a tidy resolution.

My sister has since apologized. I've received her words, and I believe they came from a sincere place. But the sting remains. The memory of that judgment, layered on top of my grief, blindsided me. It made an already unbearable moment feel even heavier.

I pray she never has to know that kind of heartbreak. I pray she never has to make that kind of choice—to protect herself from one of her own children. She has three. And I wouldn't wish that kind of pain on any of them.

The truth is, in a way, it *was* about punishment. It was tough love. I had asked my family to stand in solidarity with me—not to turn on him, but to hold a united front. To reinforce the boundaries I was forced to put in place. My younger sister did. My mother and my middle sister did not. And that broke me in a different way.

Because when you are drawing lines for your own survival, nothing hurts more than realizing those closest to you won't hold the line with you.

It was never easy. It was never simple. But it was necessary.

Addiction, anger, and misunderstanding had blurred the edges of our relationship, but never the love. That love never left me. It was there in the silence. It was there in the space. It was even there in the boundaries.

I didn't cry "I'm sorry" because I wished I'd done things differently. I cried because I wished things had been different. Because I mourned the kind of peace we never got to return to when he was my protective little boy. Because I hated that tough love had to be our last language.

I didn't need forgiveness for the way I loved him. I needed space to grieve the impossibility of loving someone so deeply while also needing to let go. I needed grace for the reality that love alone had not been enough to save him—or to save us from the heartbreak of our final chapter.

Journal Prompt:

Have you ever had to set a boundary with someone you deeply love?
Reflect on the emotions that arose—guilt, grief, peace, or even relief.
What do you wish others understood about your decision? What do
you wish you could say to that person now, with time and
perspective?

_____

_____

_____

_____

_____

Affirmation:

*I honor the boundary I made from a place of love, not punishment.
I release the shame others tried to place on me. I am allowed to
protect my peace, even when it breaks my heart.*

The Front Pew

There are things I'll never say out loud.

Not because I'm hiding, but because the pain is just that deep.

During the years my relationship with my son was strained, so much happened. Things that broke me in private. Things I carried alone out of hurt and shame. Even my closest cousin, the one who knows nearly everything, never heard the full story. And my friends? They saw the highlights—the smiling photos, the good reports—but not the reality.

So when I sat on the front pew at his funeral, just feet away from his casket, very few people knew what was really going through my mind. My body was still but my spirit was in pieces.

They didn't know I was replaying old arguments in my head.

Or wondering what might've changed if I'd said one more thing—or kept one more thing to myself.

They didn't know I was grieving two losses: the son I buried... and the version of us I'd prayed to see healed.

Journal Prompt:

Have you ever grieved something that others couldn't see—an unspoken truth, a private pain, a version of the story no one else knew?

Write about what you carried silently. What you wish others understood. What healing looks like when it happens behind the scenes.

Affirmation:

Even when my grief is invisible to others, it is valid. I honor what I've carried in silence and give myself permission to speak my truth—on my terms.

The Unspoken Grief

Grief is already heavy. But grief wrapped in secrecy? Grief tangled with shame, judgment, and all the things you never got to say? That's something else entirely.

I kept quiet because I didn't want to dishonor him.
 I didn't want people to judge him—or me.
And honestly, I didn't want to relive it all just to satisfy someone else's curiosity.
So I smiled through tears. I nodded through clichés. I carried the weight of silence like a second skin.

There's a cost to that kind of silence.

When you feel like you have to protect someone's memory, even while trying to survive their loss, it creates a grief that's hidden in plain sight. You become your own censor. You tuck the truth beneath polished sentences and avoid the parts of your story that make people uncomfortable.

You learn to comfort others with edited versions of your pain.

But that unspoken grief still shows up.

In the quiet moments.

In the anniversaries you don't mention.

In the stories you stop yourself from telling.

Naming It Now:

But I can name it here:

That silence was devastating.

That grief was complicated.

And even now, I'm learning how to let go of the things I never got to fix.

I am learning that protecting someone's dignity and telling the truth does not have to be opposites. I can love him and still name the hard parts. I can grieve him and still honor the whole truth of who he was.

And maybe, just maybe, by speaking the unspeakable—I can finally begin to heal.

Journal Prompt:

What parts of your grief have gone unspoken?
Write about the things you've carried quietly—out of fear, shame, or protection. What truths are you ready to name for your own healing, even if you never share them aloud?

_____

_____

_____

_____

_____

Affirmation:

My silence does not make me stronger. My truth is safe with me. Speaking it is not betrayal—it is release.

Misunderstood, But Still Mine

At Derrion's funeral, someone said he was misunderstood. Another spoke about offering grace to those dealing with emotional struggles. Their words hung in the air, sharp and soft all at once—like truth wrapped in tenderness.

I sat there and felt the weight of it. I knew he was hurting. I tried to reach him, love him, and guide him. But there were days I couldn't find the version of him I remembered, and days I couldn't recognize the version of me I had become in response to the chaos. In that moment, surrounded by words and grief, I wondered if I had failed him. If I had missed a moment, a signal, a need. If I had been too tired, too scared, too human.

But even in that wondering, I held one thing steady: he was mine. Through every misunderstanding, every struggle, every silence. He was mine.

And maybe grace isn't just something we offer others—it's something we have to learn to offer ourselves, especially when we're parenting through pain. I don't know if I did everything right, but I know I loved him. I know I tried. And I know that love didn't die with him. It's still here, reshaping me, calling me to forgive myself for the things I didn't know and to release the things I couldn't control.

Journal Prompt:
Reflect on a moment when you felt like you failed your child.
What would grace look like in that moment—toward them, and
toward yourself?
What do you wish others had understood about your child's
struggle?

_____

_____

_____

_____

_____

Affirmation:
I give myself grace for the things I couldn't fix.
My love was real, and my effort mattered—even when the outcome
broke my heart.

Eternal Peace

Riding around the cemetery with the funeral director felt like floating through a terrible dream—one where the air was heavy with finality, and every stop we made seemed to scream *this isn't it*. Plot after plot, nothing felt right. I wasn't just picking a place in the ground—I was searching for something sacred. Something that whispered *home* in a way that was worthy of my son.

Each section of the cemetery felt too exposed, too plain, too crowded, too ordinary. I couldn't imagine leaving him there, in places that felt like afterthoughts. My heart ached with every turn we made, frustration mounting as my soul silently screamed *this can't be where his story ends.*

Then we came upon the mausoleum section—and I saw the words "Eternal Peace." Just like that, I knew. It was like God whispered directly to me at that moment. *That's it. That's where he belongs.* My baby deserved peace—deep, sacred, undisturbed peace. A place that felt sealed in love, not sorrow.

A place that felt final in the most gentle, holy way. The best I could give him when I couldn't give him life anymore.

Eternal Peace. The words were more than a building name. They were a promise.

And I needed that promise for him—and for me.

Journal Prompt:

What moments in your grief journey have felt like divine confirmation—those times when something just clicked, and you knew it was right? How did your heart respond in those moments?

_____

_____

_____

_____

_____

Affirmation:

I believe in sacred rest. Even in the depths of grief, I trust that peace can be found—in places, in memories, and within my spirit. I release what I cannot carry and make room for healing that is quiet, holy, and complete.

Sunflower Goodbye

I will never forget the moment they placed his coffin into the crypt. My knees didn't buckle, but something inside me did.

On top of the casket was my favorite flower—a sunflower. Bright. Bold. Always turning its face toward the sun, even on the darkest days.

It felt symbolic, intentional, and sacred. That sunflower was my last gift to him. And in that moment, as I watched his body be sealed away from this world, I whispered a prayer I had whispered so many times before, but never with such finality:

God, please take care of my baby.

It was the most helpless, holy moment of my life. There was nothing else I could do. No more protecting, no more parenting, no more pleading. Just surrender.

That day, the sunflower was more than just a flower. It was a prayer in bloom. A symbol of the love I will carry as long as I live.

Journal Prompt:

Think back to the funeral or memorial service. What image or moment is frozen in your memory? What did you say, feel, or pray at that moment—and how does it still echo in your heart today?

_____

_____

_____

_____

Affirmation:

Even when I could no longer hold him, my love reached him. My prayers still do.

Prayer/Transition: A Prayer in the In-Between

God, meet me in the shift. Between memory and finality, between the son I still hold and the one I had to let go, steady my heart. Let every decision made in sorrow be wrapped in sacred peace. And let my love, somehow, be enough to guide us all the way through.

Two Sons, One Loss

Grief has a way of narrowing your vision. The pain becomes so loud, so thick, that it fills the room and mutes everything else. In my sorrow over losing Derrion, I've sometimes forgotten that I didn't lose him alone. His brother did, too.

My surviving son, Cameron, didn't just lose a sibling. He lost a friend, a history, a shared language only brothers know. And while I've been sitting in my own ache, I wonder if he's been quietly carrying his. I worry that I've been too consumed with my own grief to recognize his. And with that worry comes guilt. Am I failing him, too?

But then I breathe and remember this: I am not perfect, but I am present. Maybe I haven't always had the right words. Maybe I've missed some moments. But I'm still here. And there is still time to show up differently. To ask how he's doing. To sit with his memories. To say, "I miss him too. I miss him with you."

The truth is, Derrion had been unraveling emotionally long before he was introduced to anything stronger than marijuana. As a teenager, he carried the heavy ache of abandonment after his father disappeared without a trace for five years. I saw the confusion in his eyes, the way his spirit dimmed, and I took him to a therapist because I knew I couldn't carry that weight for him—but I wanted to at least help him name it.

He was so stubborn. So angry. He wouldn't let the therapist help him. He'd just sit there and stare, not saying a word. This went on for three sessions before I stopped sending him. I'll never forget the therapist telling Derrion he could see the Cherokee blood in his features—his grandmother was part Native American. At the time, I think the therapist was trying to name something unspoken: a bloodline of addiction, a legacy of suppressed rage. Whether Derrion understood the weight of those words or not, I'm not sure. But I heard them. And I've never forgotten.

Cameron and I are both navigating this loss, just in different ways. And maybe the bridge between our grief is not perfection—but presence, patience, and love.

Journal Prompt:
How has your surviving child experienced this loss? What do you think he needs most from you right now—not as a perfect parent, but as a grieving mother who is still choosing to love, even through the pain?

_____

_____

_____

_____

Affirmation:
Even in my sorrow, I can make room for the grief of others. I am not failing—I am finding my way back to connection, one moment at a time.

A Letter to Cameron

My Dearest Cameron,

I need to start with the most important thing: I see you.

We've always shared something sacred, this closeness, this unspoken rhythm that's kept us side by side through so many seasons. When Derrion passed, I didn't retreat or shut down. I stayed present, but if I'm being honest, I don't think I asked you enough about how *you* were really doing.

Everything felt so heavy, so new, so unwelcome. I was wading through my own grief and trying to make sense of a world that no longer felt familiar. But even in all that, I never stopped protecting you, just like I always have. Even when it meant guarding your heart from the storm your brother sometimes brought with him.

You didn't just lose a brother. You lost someone who mirrored your memories, who understood your inside jokes and your childhood language. The kind of loss that's hard to explain but even harder to carry. I know it's yours, and I want you to know that I haven't overlooked it, even if I didn't say enough.

And then, when life knocked us off balance again with your illness, I felt that fear rise up in me all over again. ***Not both of them, God. Please... not both.***

It reminded me that silence is not always strength. Some things need to be said.

So here's what I want you to hear:

You are not alone in this grief.

I miss him too. I miss him with you. I still hear the echoes of your shared laughter, and I see glimpses of him in the way you move, the way you love, the way you keep going.

But hear this too,

You are not in his shadow.

You've always been a light of your own.

Even when I've been quiet, your strength has held me together in ways I can't explain.

Watching you father Suede with patience, humor, and love fills my heart in a way that words can't fully express. Your presence in his life is powerful. You are breaking cycles, building bonds, and doing what matters most: showing up.

I don't always know the right words to say, but I'm here. I want to remember him with you, laugh at the things only the two of you understood, cry when it hurts too much, and honor what you lost without ever making you feel like you have to carry mine too.

We're both still figuring out how to live with this loss, but we don't have to do it separately.

You are mine. I love you. I always will.

Love,

Momma

Part III: Living With Loss

"I am still learning how to live with what I'll never get back, and love what I still have."
—Misty Reshun

Grief doesn't leave. It simply changes its shape. These pages carry the echoes of a life now lived alongside absence. In this space, I share what it means to wake up without the person you prayed for, and still find reasons to keep going. It is not about moving on. It's about learning how to move differently.

- Included Titles:

  - Sometimes I Pretend He's Just Locked Up
  - Grief Changed the Way I Relate to People
  - Grief Made Me Need Less Noise and More Truth
  - The Grief Between Us
  - Juxtaposition
  - The Drug That Shattered the Calm
  - When They Ask How Many Children I Have
  - The Invisible Jet
  - Parenting After the Shield Shattered
  - Reflection: Prayers with my Guard Up
  - Two Truths Can Exist
  - Unchosen Sisterhood
  - Milestones Without Him

Sometimes I Pretend He's Just Locked Up

There are days when I can almost convince myself that Derrion is just incarcerated again. That he's not gone forever—just temporarily out of reach. That he'll call eventually. That I'll visit. That I'll hear his voice through glass and wait for the day he comes home.

It's strange, isn't it? That grief can twist time like that. That my brain, in trying to protect me, sometimes slips into a place where loss feels like a sentence instead of a final goodbye.

I remember visiting Derrion once when he was in jail in Louisiana. I sat across from him, doing my best to hold myself together. Next to us, another mother sat with her son. I heard her say something to her son that stuck with me:

"I'm just glad you are in here. At least I know where you are."

Derrion was stunned. "Man, that's messed up!" he said, shaking his head.

But I looked at him and said something I think he wasn't ready to hear:

"I completely understand how she feels. I feel the same way."

He couldn't fathom that. Couldn't grasp how a mother could find peace in seeing her son behind bars.

But for some of us—mothers of sons who struggle—there's a strange comfort in knowing they're alive. Safe. Not out in the chaos. Not a phone call away from tragedy.

And now, I would give anything for a phone call. Even from jail.

Because jail wasn't the end. It wasn't forever.

But this? This grief? This silence?

This is forever.

So sometimes I let myself pretend. Just for a minute. That he's away. That he'll be home. That we're just waiting for time to pass.

Journal Prompt:

Have you ever caught yourself pretending your loved one is "just away"—incarcerated, traveling, busy—but not gone? What does that reveal about the ways your mind and heart are coping? Write about a memory, like a visit or phone call, that sticks with you. What did you hear, see, feel in that moment that still echoes today?

You might begin with:
• *Sometimes I imagine that...*
• *I remember when we...*
• *What I said that day still feels...*
• *What I wish I could tell him now is...*

_____

_____

_____

_____

_____

Affirmation:
It's okay to long for the familiar—even the painful parts—when the alternative is permanent loss. My mind is trying to protect my heart, and that's its own kind of love.

Grief Changed the Way I Relate to People

When I lost Derrion, I didn't just lose him.

I lost the version of me that existed before the loss.

And because of that, many of my relationships changed, too.

Some people showed up like angels—silent, steady, loving. They brought food. Sat in the quiet with me. Checked in even after the flowers faded. I'll never forget that kind of love.

But others... disappeared.

And what hurts most is who disappeared.

People I never would have questioned.

People I thought would be by my side no matter what.

My former pastor? Silent.

My church family—the same people I worshiped with, prayed with, served with? Gone.

My stepdaughter from my marriage? Not a word.

It's hard not to tie it to my decision to leave my marriage. To wonder if my grief was somehow disqualified in their eyes because of a choice they didn't agree with. As if losing my son didn't "count" the same because I didn't stay in a situation that was no longer right for me.

That silence felt like judgment.
That absence felt like rejection.
And that hurt added another layer to a heart already broken.

Grief revealed who could sit with pain without trying to control the narrative.

But even in that pain, I've also seen light.

I've formed new bonds with people who met me where I was—with no agenda, no assumptions, just presence. There's something sacred about being seen in sorrow. Something healing about being able to say, "I'm not okay," and being met with, "That's okay."

Grief didn't just break me—it redefined me.
And the people who are still standing with me now? They've met the real me.
The raw me. The reshaped me. The one who doesn't need a pulpit to be worthy of love.

Journal Prompt:

Who surprised you with their presence—or their absence—during your grief? What did that shift teach you about the kind of support you need, and the kind of relationships you value most?

_____

_____

_____

_____

_____

Affirmation:

I release the people who chose absence. Their silence is not my shame. I am loved, worthy, and seen—exactly as I am.

Grief Made Me Need Less Noise and More Truth

Grief stripped me of my tolerance for small talk, fake smiles, and surface-level connections. It made me crave quiet—not silence, but stillness. The kind of peace that lets you hear your own heart beat and recognize your own pain without distraction.

I used to surround myself with people, music, movement—anything that filled the air. But after Derrion passed, all that noise felt like a weight I couldn't carry. I didn't want chatter, I wanted connection. I didn't want sympathy, I wanted sincerity.

Grief became a filter. It helped me see who could sit with my sorrow without trying to fix it. Who could handle the truth without looking away. Who could love the raw version of me, not just the strong one.

Now, I seek truth. Real conversations. Quiet support. Sacred presence. I don't need crowds. I need people who come with peace, not performance.

Journal Prompt:

Who do you feel most yourself around—the real, grieving, still-healing you? What kinds of spaces make you feel seen and safe?

_____

_____

_____

_____

_____

Affirmation:

I am allowed to choose peace over performance. My healing requires truth, not noise.

The Grief Between Us

After losing Derrion, the ache in my heart was immediate and consuming, but I knew I wasn't the only one carrying it. My son Cameron was grieving too. His pain wasn't loud, but it was there—steady and deep. He lost his brother. Not just someone who shared a room, but someone who shared his past, his perspective, and pieces of his story no one else fully understood.

Their relationship wasn't perfect. There were battles and misunderstandings. But it was real. It was brotherhood. And when Derrion died, a part of Cameron's world shifted too.

There's no blueprint for parenting after loss. I didn't ignore his grief, but I also didn't always know how to hold it alongside my own. We were both navigating unfamiliar ground—me as a mother learning to show up with empty arms, him as a brother carrying memories and questions that no one else could fully answer. Some days, the silence between us felt heavy. Not from a lack of love, but from the weight of grief we didn't know how to share.

But the grief between us wasn't just about me and Cameron.

Derrion's father was grieving too, though his grief showed up differently—drenched in self-pity and regret. Instead of drawing us together, it widened the space between us. While I was making calls, choosing caskets, and trying to honor our son's memory, he was unreachable—both physically and emotionally. His sorrow consumed him to the point that he couldn't find his way to Texas to help. He didn't stand beside me in those days that felt impossible. He simply showed up the day before the funeral—too late to help carry the weight, too lost in his own pain to offer anything more than presence.

And yet, even presence can feel like absence when the chasm between two people is that wide.

We were all grieving—but not together. That's the cruel trick of grief. It isolates. It rearranges the ways we show up for each other. It silences the people we need most and makes the ones who try feel like strangers. I used to think grief could be a bridge, but sometimes, it's a wall. And we all end up on different sides, staring through the cracks, wondering how to reach one another.

What I know now is that love can stretch. It can rise above the silence, above the sorrow, and say, *"I see you."* Cameron's grief may look different than mine. His father's grief may have taken a different path. But none of it is insignificant.

Even if the grief between us never fully closes, I want those I love to know this: Your pain is real. Your story matters. And no matter how broken or distant we may feel, love still lives here—trying, reaching, healing.

Journal Prompt:
Think of a time when grief created distance between you and someone you love. What went unsaid? What did you need that you didn't receive—and what were you unable to give? Reflect on how grief has shaped your ability to connect or disconnect with others. Are there bridges worth rebuilding, or boundaries that still serve you? Honor your truth without judgment.

_____

_____

_____

_____

_____

Affirmation:
I honor the quiet grief of those who remain. There is space in my love for every story, every sorrow, and every survivor.

Juxtaposition

On the second anniversary of Derrion's death, I posted something on social media that echoed the tangled mess of emotions I had been silently carrying:

"Trying to heal, while trying to grieve, while trying to live, while trying to forgive, while trying to love."

That sentence wrapped its arms around me. It put words to the weight I had been dragging behind my smile.

My life felt like a contradiction.

Scroll through my social media and you'll see snapshots of joy—travel, adventure, laughter with family and friends. But those images never told the whole truth. Behind every picture was a heart in turmoil, trying to balance living with loss. I was grieving and smiling. Mourning and dancing. Loving others while struggling to love myself.

I didn't want pity—I just wanted peace.

But peace felt so far away when I was doing all the "tryings" at once.

Journal Prompt:

In what ways does your outer life mask your inner reality? What would it feel like to be seen fully—not just in joy, but in your sorrow too?

_____

_____

_____

_____

_____

Affirmation:

I give myself permission to hold joy and grief at the same time. Both are real. Both are mine. Both deserve space.

The Drug That Shattered the Calm

I've written around it. Danced near the truth. Hinted at what lurked beneath the chaos. But I haven't said it outright. Not in the way it deserves to be said.

It wasn't just "addiction."
 It was PCP. "Wet". That's what they call it in the streets.

I remember the moment everything shifted. My phone rang. It was my mother—frantic, screaming, pleading with Derrion not to ransack her home. I sped over, panic driving every breath. When I pulled up, his "favorite" cousin met me in the yard. That's when he told me: He smoked something laced. PCP. That street drug that drags people into madness.

PCP, or phencyclidine, is a dissociative drug. Originally developed as an anesthetic, it was pulled from medical use because it triggered psychosis, rage, and hallucinations. On the street, it's called "Wet"—often marijuana or cigarettes dipped in embalming fluid laced with PCP.

It doesn't just alter perception. It hijacks the mind. And it was hijacking my son.

I walked into the room and tried to calm him. I kept my voice soft, steady. I looked into his eyes—those same eyes I once memorized when he was swaddled in my arms. But what I saw that day didn't belong to my son. His eyes looked almost... demonic. Cold. Vacant. Wild.

It was the most frightening experience I've ever had as a mother. I wasn't afraid of him. I was afraid for him. Afraid of what the drug had done. Afraid of what might come next.

No, he didn't die from the drug. He drowned. But the drug—that drug—killed our relationship slowly, over the next dreadful years. It chipped away at his spirit, his logic, his compassion. It robbed us of trust. Of ease. Of connection. I never knew who I'd be dealing with. The sweet, funny son I raised? Or the unpredictable man shaped by a haze of hallucinations and heartbreak?

PCP doesn't just break the person who smokes it. It breaks everything around them:

- The mother who prays herself numb.

- The siblings who stop answering calls.

- The grandmother who shakes in her own home.

- The woman who loved him until it became dangerous.

No one talks enough about the grief that comes before the death. The grief of watching someone unravel while you're still trying to hold them close. Still trying to save what's slipping away.

I may never know what he was trying to escape. What hurt he was trying to numb. But what I do know is that from the moment I walked into that room—calm voice, trembling hands, pleading heart—everything changed.

And nothing was ever the same.

Journal Prompt:

Have you ever experienced a moment when someone you loved felt unreachable or changed in a way you couldn't explain? What did that moment do to your sense of safety, connection, or identity? Write about the grief that comes *before* the loss—the slow unraveling, the moments you tried to hold on, and what you had to release in order to survive.

Affirmation:

I release the guilt of not being able to save someone I love from their own spiral. I honor the truth of what I endured, even when others do not see it. My love was real. My fear was valid. My boundaries were necessary. I am healing, even from the parts I rarely speak about.

When They Ask How Many Children I Have

There's a question that feels harmless to most people.

A casual part of small talk.

"How many children do you have?"

Now, It sneaks up on me in the most ordinary moments—

At work, during icebreakers.

At social gatherings, when strangers are trying to find a connection.

Sometimes at church, when someone is just trying to make conversation.

But for me, it's never just a question.

It's a wound. A quiet calculation. A silent storm.

Because I don't know how to answer.

Do I say I have two sons? Because I do.

Do I say one son, and one who passed away?

Do I let my silence hang in the air while my mind spirals?

I never imagined how loaded that question could be—

Not until I became the mother of a child I could no longer touch.

Before Derrion died, I understood that question as neutral.

Now, I see it as a trap wrapped in politeness.

And yet, I've asked it too.

I've asked people if they have children.

I've navigated awkward pauses when someone said no.

But I never considered that silence could also mean:

I did, once.

I still do, but it hurts to talk about.

I'm trying not to cry right now.

I didn't understand how sensitive that question could be—

Until it broke me.

And now, even Mother's Day feels like a minefield.

I scan faces, trying to decipher if someone is a mother.

Trying to decide who to say it to.

Wondering how many women are holding invisible grief—

Because what does a mother who lost a child look like?

She looks like me.

She looks like you.

She looks like any of us.

We walk around answering impossible questions with polite smiles.

We dodge the pain in public and carry it in private.

And still—we mother.

We remember.

We love beyond the silence.

I may never have a simple answer again,

But I will always have two sons.

Even if one now lives only in memory.

Journal Prompt:

How do you answer when someone asks about your family? Write about the moments when that question has hurt, confused, or challenged you. What would it feel like to answer honestly, even if it makes others uncomfortable?

_____

_____

_____

_____

_____

Affirmation:

I honor the love I carry and the loss I live with. My story does not require explanation, only compassion—especially from myself.

The Invisible Jet

When I was a little girl, I loved watching Wonder Woman soar through the sky in her invisible jet. To me, it was the ultimate shield—strong, silent, and always present.

As a mother, I tried to create that same shield for my children, not made of metal or magic, but of prayer. I covered them daily, trusting those prayers to protect them, to surround them in hope and safety, with the expectation of a long and fruitful life.

I never imagined I would bury a child.

When Derrion passed, it felt like that invisible shield shattered. The protection I thought I had—the faith I clung to so tightly—was pierced by a grief I couldn't have prepared for. I lost more than a son that day. I lost the unshakable belief that I could somehow keep them safe through sheer love and faith.

I don't know if I'll ever believe the same way again.

But I still believe in love. I still believe in prayer. And I still believe that even in the brokenness, God meets me here.

Reflection Prompt:

What was your "invisible jet"—the thing you believed could protect your child or your heart? What has changed now, and how are you holding that shift?

_____

_____

_____

_____

_____

Affirmation:

Even in the ruins of what I once believed, I honor my love, my grief, and the strength it takes to still be here.

Parenting After the Shield Shattered

When Derrion died, something inside me shifted forever. The invisible shield I believed I had—the one I thought protected my children through love, faith, and prayer—was broken.

And when that shield broke, so did a part of me.

Now, I parent my remaining son differently.

Not out of fear, but with a deeper awareness that I *cannot* protect him from everything. That the unthinkable is, in fact, thinkable.

That grief can come knocking when you least expect it.

I hold him a little closer, but I also let go a little more.

Because I know that control is an illusion—but love, when given freely, is not.

And then there are my grandchildren—especially Derrion's children.

I show up for them in ways I couldn't always show up for their father.

I wonder what they'll carry. What they'll remember.

I wonder how his absence, and the truth of his addiction and pain, will shape their story.

Sometimes I ask God if taking Derrion was, in some divine and heartbreaking way, a form of protection—for them, and maybe even for him.

Would his brokenness have left deeper scars if he had stayed?
Would his addiction have made him someone they feared instead of missed?

These are questions without answers.
But I carry them in my chest like smooth stones—heavy, but worn by prayer.

So now, I grandparent with intention.
I create joy on purpose. I speak life. I leave room for the hard conversations. I say his name. I let them see my tears.
I try to be a soft place for them to land—because grief took my shield, but it didn't take my heart.

Journal Prompt:

How has loss changed the way you love and show up for the people still here? What have you learned about presence now that you've lived through absence?

_____

_____

_____

_____

_____

Affirmation:

Even after loss, I remain a vessel of love. I show up fully—broken and whole—for the ones who still need me.

Prayers with My Guard Up

There was a time when I prayed like I was negotiating with God. I had requests, expectations, and promises. I wanted my will to be honored—for my son to change, live, and come back to himself. To come back to me.

But grief humbled my prayers.

Now, I pray with my guard up—not against God, but against false expectations. I don't demand. I surrender. I say, "Not my will, but Yours." And I mean it. Because I've learned that love doesn't always equal the outcome I want. Healing doesn't always look the way I pictured.

This kind of prayer is quieter. Wiser. Sometimes wordless. But it's no less sacred. Because even when my guard is up, my heart is still open.

Journal Prompt:

How have your prayers or spiritual conversations changed since your loss? What do you say differently now?

_____

_____

_____

_____

_____

Affirmation:

Even when I pray with caution, I still pray with love. I trust what I cannot yet see.

Two Truths Can Exist

"You can hold two truths at once: Your parents did their best, AND their best might have hurt you."

That statement found me at a time when I was starting to unpeel layers I didn't even know I was carrying. And it sat with me. Sat *in* me. Because I've lived it from both sides.

I became a mother at 18. A baby raising a baby, full of love and fear and grit. I didn't know what I didn't know. I didn't grow up fathered — that absence was loud. But I was mothered. My mama had me at 21, and she poured into me the best of what she had. I never felt unloved. Never felt unmothered. But now, with time and tenderness, I can see that *her* best came from what *she* had been given — and maybe that wasn't always complete.

The older I get, the more I understand how cycles repeat not because we don't care, but because we don't know better until life or love or loss teaches us. I wonder sometimes if Derrion saw me that way.

A young mother doing her best. A woman trying to love through pain, still learning how to hold her own wounds.

This isn't about blame. It's about truth-telling. It's about making room for grace — for them, for me, for him. Two truths can live in the same breath. I did my best. And my best might have hurt him. My mother did her best. And some of that hurt me, too. I can hold all of it. And I will — so I can help break what needs breaking, and heal what's still tender.

Journal Prompt:

What did young motherhood teach you about love, limits, and legacy? In what ways were you mothered well — and in what ways did you long for more? What does it mean to forgive someone for being human, not perfect?

_____

_____

_____

_____

Affirmation:

I honor the love that raised me, even as I heal from the parts that missed me. I am both the fruit and the gardener. I tend to myself with truth and tenderness.

Unchosen Sisterhood

There was a time when I dreamed of wearing the pink and green.

Of strolling across a stage with my sisters, bonded by legacy, excellence, and service.

Of becoming a proud member of Alpha Kappa Alpha Sorority, Inc.— the first sorority established by and for Black women.

That dream never faded, even as the years passed.

But life happened. Work, motherhood, time, requirements, gatekeeping.

Post-graduate membership proved to be a harder path than I imagined.

Still, I held onto hope.

There was something sacred to me about belonging to a sisterhood rooted in tradition, dignity, and purpose.

And then one day, everything changed.

When Derrion passed, I was initiated into a sisterhood I never asked to join.

A sacred, sorrowful, unseen society.

Mothers who have buried their children.

Women who wake up every day with a part of their heart missing, who carry both love and grief in their bones.

Who cry in the shower, smile in public, and pray to just make it through another day.

No ceremony. No colors. No step shows.

Just quiet nods of knowing.

Tears that fall without explanation.

And an unspoken understanding that we are forever changed.

This is not the sisterhood I dreamed of.

But it is one I now honor.

Because these women, these grieving mothers, are some of the strongest souls I've ever known.

They don't wear letters across their chest,

but they carry a different kind of badge—

one of love that never ends,

grief that reshapes everything,

and courage that defies reason.

One day, I may still become a member of Alpha Kappa Alpha.

But no matter what, I will always be part of this unchosen

sisterhood.

And I vow to honor our stories,

speak our names,

and lift one another up—

because only we know what it means to survive this kind of loss.

Journal Prompt:

Have you ever found yourself part of a "group" or season of life you never envisioned? How did that unexpected belonging shape you—your faith, your relationships, your view of yourself?

_____

_____

_____

_____

Affirmation:

I honor the sisterhood I never asked for, and the strength I never imagined I would need. Though grief chose me, I chose to carry love forward—one breath, one memory, one day at a time.

Milestones Without Him

It's not just the big loss.

It's all the little ones that follow.

Every milestone, every celebration, every new chapter, every proud moment carries a shadow. A pause. A sting.

When Dez graduated from Pre-K, I smiled for the pictures. Clapped, cheered, and beamed with MiMi pride. But inside, I couldn't help thinking: Derrion should be here. He would've been so proud. Probably making silly jokes or calling me to brag about his son, in that way only he could. I wanted to hear his voice in that crowd, just once more.

Then came Dez's first football game.

Football was Derrion's thing. He loved it so much he carried a ball with him everywhere like it was part of him. He could turn anything into a game, a moment of joy, a reason to run and laugh and shine.

Watching Dez on that field, I saw echoes of him. His spirit. His passion. His love for the game.

And I also felt the hole. The "what if." The "he should've been here."

Even when my niece, Derrion's cousin, graduated from college, I felt it. She followed the tradition of jumping into the river with the other graduates, fully dressed, and full of joy. It was a beautiful, wild moment. But I couldn't help wondering how proud Derrion would've been. What kind of advice he would've given her? What jokes he would've made afterward.

The truth is, these moments are bittersweet now.

Grief is braided into every celebration.

Joy doesn't erase the sorrow. It sits beside it.

And I'm learning to hold both.

Journal Prompt:

Think about a milestone you recently experienced without your loved one present. What made you smile? What made you ache? How do you carry their memory with you into these moments? What would you say to them if they had been there?

_____

_____

_____

_____

_____

Affirmation:

I honor every milestone with love, even when it hurts. My joy and grief can coexist. My celebration can carry memories. My heart can hold both sorrow and pride.

Part IV: Boundaries, Forgiveness & Becoming

"Loving someone doesn't always mean staying close. Sometimes, it means choosing peace, even when it aches."
—Misty Reshun

Healing asked more of me than I expected. It asked me to release guilt, reclaim peace, and stop carrying people who didn't want to be held. This section is where I started choosing myself—where I realized that becoming whole sometimes means stepping back, letting go, and loving from afar.

- Included Titles:

  - The Boundary I Never Thought Would Be the Last
  - Forgiveness With Fences
  - Forgiveness ≠ Reconciliation
  - The Space Between Brothers
  - The Boundary Line
  - You'll Understand It Better By and By

The Boundary I Never Thought Would Be the Last

People talk about setting boundaries like it's a healthy milestone—and it is. But what no one talks about is the emotional aftermath, the silent fear, the what-ifs. It usually takes people a while to get to that point, to say, *"I can't keep doing this."* But no one ever thinks the boundary might become final.

As a parent, there's always hope tucked in the corner of your resolve. Hope that by choosing yourself—your peace, your sanity—it will show the other person your worth. Hope that they'll see the line you drew and finally change course. Hope for some kind of recompense, even if it's just an honest conversation, an apology, or a moment of clarity.

The last time I set a boundary with my son, I remained steadfast. There were no calls, no texts, and nothing for over 365 days.

And then he called.

It was a week before he passed. He left a voicemail asking for my help with a legal matter—just like before. And at the end, he said, *"I love you."*

Not *"I'm sorry for how I acted the last time we saw each other."*
Not *"I shouldn't have said those things."*
Just *"Mom, I need your help... I love you."*

My text response was short: *"I'm sorry, but I'm unable to help you. I wish you well."*

And that was it.

As a mother, that is haunting. My maternal instincts don't make me that cold. But the years of pain, manipulation, and emotional exhaustion had brought me to a place I never imagined. "How did things get to the point where I felt I had no choice?" I'll forever be devastated by the timing. The silence. The finality.

I didn't know that was the last time I would hear him say *Momma*.

Journal Prompt:

Have you ever had to set a boundary that felt both necessary and painful? What led up to that decision? What emotions surface when you think about the last interaction with your child (or loved one)? Write down what you wish you could say, without editing or judgment. If your boundary became final—how do you hold both the grief and the self-respect? Reflect on a moment when you honored your own needs. What did it cost you? What did it preserve? How do you define forgiveness when there is no apology? What do you need to say to your inner mother/father/caregiver today, at this very moment?

Affirmation:

I honor the courage it took to protect myself, even when it broke my heart. I can love deeply and still have limits. I will not silence my pain, but I will not drown in it either. Even in devastation, I deserve grace.

Forgiveness with Fences

Grief has a way of forcing you to sit with things you thought you could avoid—like forgiveness.

I didn't forgive Derrion while he was alive.

The pain was too fresh, the wounds too raw. We were both hurting, both protecting ourselves in ways that only added to the distance between us. And then... he was gone.

For a long time after, I held onto that pain. I cycled through the "what ifs," the regrets, the conversations we never finished.

The apology I never received.
The one I never gave.

It took over a year after he passed for me to even consider forgiveness. I had to do it without hearing the words I longed for. I had to find a way to forgive him in the silence.

And maybe... just maybe... his last call, asking for help, was his way of apologizing. Maybe that was all he could offer in that moment.

I replay it often—wondering if I missed the message hidden in his voice.

Forgiveness came slowly. Quietly.

Not in a big, dramatic release, but in tiny moments where I chose peace over resentment. Where I let go of needing to understand everything. Now I forgive with fences.

I forgive to free myself, not to erase the past or open the door. Forgiveness doesn't mean there's no boundary—it just means the bitterness doesn't run the show anymore.

I forgive, not to forget, but to free myself.

Journal Prompt:

What do you need to forgive someone who can no longer say "I'm sorry"? Can you find peace even in the absence of closure?

_____

_____

_____

_____

_____

Affirmation:

I offer forgiveness as a gift to myself. I can heal, even without the words I wanted to hear. Peace is mine to claim.

Forgiveness ≠ Reconciliation

For a long time, I believed that if I truly forgave someone, it meant I had to let them back in. That forgiveness required a return to "normal," a healed relationship, a reunion of sorts.

But grief has changed my lens.

I've learned that forgiveness and reconciliation are not synonymous.

One is about my heart.

The other is about relationships.

Forgiveness is deeply personal. It's something I do to release myself from anger, guilt, or resentment. It's how I unclench my fist so I can breathe again.

Reconciliation, on the other hand, requires two willing people. It requires safety, accountability, and honesty—and in some cases, it requires change that simply never comes.

So now, I forgive people who may never know they hurt me.

I forgive those who aren't safe to let back in.

I forgive not to mend the bond, but to mend me.

Some doors will remain closed—not out of spite, but out of wisdom.

And that doesn't make my forgiveness any less real.

It just makes it more sacred.

Journal Prompt:

Have you ever confused forgiveness with reconciliation? What relationships in your life have taught you the difference?

_____

_____

_____

_____

Affirmation:

I can forgive without reconnecting. I can heal without reopening old wounds. My peace does not depend on anyone else's participation.

The Space Between Brothers

When Derrion became a teenager and started to stray—experimenting with drugs and running with the wrong crowd—I felt an urgent need to protect Cameron. That protection meant creating distance between them. I couldn't let them hang out together, not because I loved one more than the other, but because I had to shield Cameron from what I couldn't yet stop in Derrion.

Derrion felt it, though. That space. And to him, it looked like favoritism. It looked like rejection. What it was—was survival. What it became—was a misunderstanding.

As Cameron got older and I trusted that he could protect his heart and his boundaries, I let them share space again occasionally. There were good moments. But in the later years of Derrion's addiction, things turned dark. They had a physical altercation—one that cut deep and scarred Cameron in ways that only therapy helped unravel. That's the part people don't always see.

Addiction doesn't just touch the person using. It touches everyone around them.

This is not just a parent-child issue. It's a sibling issue. A family issue. It's about what gets passed around when love gets interrupted by pain.

Journal Prompt:

How have you seen one child impacted by the pain or choices of another? What protective instincts have shaped your parenting? What does forgiveness look like within sibling relationships? Within yourself?

_____

_____

_____

_____

_____

Affirmation:

I did what I had to do to protect the one who still respected me. I honor both of my sons—the one I lost and the one who stayed.

The Boundary Line

Before grief, I used to wrestle with boundaries. I worried about hurting people's feelings, being misunderstood, or appearing cold. I gave second, third, and even tenth chances—especially to people I loved.

I had set boundaries in the past with Derrion. This wasn't the first time we went a span without talking. In those earlier times, we would just fall back into our mother-son rhythm without a formal apology. We loved each other, and that was enough to reset things. But the last altercation was so massive, so deeply disrespectful, that I had to stand my ground.

Something changed after Derrion passed.

When I was forced to accept a boundary between me and my own child—through death, estrangement, and heartbreak—I realized I was capable of drawing a line in the sand and not crossing it. I had no choice. That invisible thread between us had been stretched, strained, and ultimately severed, not by my desire but by circumstance and pain.

So now, when it comes to other relationships, I don't hesitate. I don't over-explain. I don't chase after closure. Because if I could accept a boundary with my flesh and blood, then it's a no-brainer with anyone else.

But I'll be honest—sometimes I wonder if I've become callous.

Have I traded compassion for self-preservation?

Am I guarding my peace... or just avoiding new wounds?

Grief changed my boundaries. And I'm still figuring out if that change is healing me or hardening me.

That final boundary redefined all others.

Journal Prompt:

Where in your life have you had to enforce a boundary that others didn't understand? How did that boundary protect you, and what did it cost you emotionally?

_____

_____

_____

_____

Affirmation:

I honor the boundaries I've had to build, even the ones forged through heartbreak. I trust that protecting my peace is not the same as closing my heart.

You'll Understand It Better By and By

There's a saying I've heard all my life: *"Just keep living. You'll understand it better by and by."*

I didn't truly grasp what it meant—until life gave me reasons to.

When I first heard the famous singer Marvin Gaye was killed by his own father, I couldn't wrap my mind around it. I thought, *How could a parent ever?* It felt unimaginable. Cold. Beyond comprehension.

But life has a way of rewriting your understanding.

The last time I saw Derrion alive, we were in the middle of the worst altercation we had ever had—a verbal fight that turned physical. Rage and heartbreak collided in that room, each of us unraveling in real-time. I remember spotting a duffle bag on the floor. I knew exactly what was in it. A gun.

And for a split second, the thought crossed my mind.

But then the rule surfaced: *If you pull it, you must be prepared to use it.*

Even amid that chaos, something deeper—something motherly, something moral—rose up and pulled me back from the edge. I thank God for that pause. For that breath. For that moment of clarity that saved us both.

It's not that I ever wanted to harm my child. It's that pain and helplessness can distort everything you think you know about yourself. Until you've stood in that kind of storm, you can't judge it. But if you keep living, if you've been bruised enough by life and love—you start to understand things you once couldn't.

And now, when I hear that old saying again, I nod. I understand—by and by.

Journal Prompt:

Write about a moment where you surprised yourself—either by the depth of your rage or the strength of your restraint. What did you learn about yourself in that moment? What do you understand now that you didn't then?

_____

_____

_____

_____

_____

Affirmation:

Even in the moments I came close to the edge, I chose life. I chose love. I am still choosing.

Part V: Life With MiMi

"MiMi is who I became when love needed a second chance to bloom."
—Misty Reshun

Becoming MiMi was always part of the plan. However, I didn't imagine holding both grief and joy in the same arms or finding new pieces of myself in the laughter of my grandchildren. But here I am—mending what was broken, not by replacing the love I lost, but by expanding the space it left behind. This part of the journey is softer. Slower. Sacred.

- Included Titles:

  - The Grandmother Grief Made Me
  - When a Child Misses Someone He Barely Knew
  - Letter to Derrion: Dez's First Football Game
  - A Note I Can't Ignore
  - The MiMi Manifesto

The Grandmother Grief Made Me

Grief may have broken something in me, but becoming MiMi stitched a part of me back together.

Dezmon, Derrion Jr., Suede, and Za'Niyah don't know the full weight I carry, and I pray they never have to. They bring light into my life in a way that feels both sacred and healing. They don't realize it, but they save me in small ways every day—with their laughter, their questions, their hugs, and the way they say "MiMi" like it's a soft place to land.

Life with MiMi is spontaneous joy.
It's singing in the car, dance battles in the living room, snacks they don't need, and stories they'll always remember.
It's making memories they'll cherish and creating a legacy bigger than pain.

They remind me to be present.
To smile on days when it would be easier to retreat.

To take pictures, plan adventures, and show up with my whole heart—even when it's heavy.

When I travel with them, when I see the world through their eyes, something inside me loosens. I realize I'm still here for a reason.

I lost a son, but I gained a renewed purpose: to pour love into the next generation and show them what it means to live boldly, love deeply, and always come back to joy.

They are part of Derrion's story, too. His fingerprints live in Dez & Derry J's faces, their energy, and sometimes even their questions. I speak his name not to anchor us in grief, but to help them remember where they come from—and how fiercely they are loved.

Journal Prompt:
Who or what in your life brings unexpected healing? How do your roles—like parent, grandparent, friend—give you new ways to reclaim joy?

_____

_____

_____

_____

_____

Affirmation:
In loving them, I am healing me. I honor the past, but I live for the present—and I find joy in every "MiMi" moment.

When a Child Misses Someone He Barely Knew

Dezmon was only a toddler when Derrion passed. He doesn't remember his father's voice, his scent, or how it felt to be wrapped in his arms. What he remembers are pictures, videos, and the stories we've chosen to keep alive for him.

The other day, I overheard him tell his sister, Za'Niyah, that he wants to die so he can go to heaven and see his dad. He said it with a soft, matter-of-fact innocence that felt like it split something open in me. Grief isn't supposed to belong to children. But here it is, curling itself around a six-year-old heart, teaching him about absence before he's even mastered tying his shoes.

I told him what I could. That his dad is with him—in his heart, in the ways he laughs, in the shape of his eyes. I told him I would be so sad if anything ever happened to him. But what I couldn't say out loud, at least not right then, is how much it hurt to hear that longing in his voice. How unfair it is that he's inherited grief he didn't choose, a hole he can't even name.

Sometimes, the most painful part of loss is watching it echo through the next generation—through a child who wants answers, connection, and comfort you can't always give. But I will keep trying. I will keep telling the stories. I will keep reminding him that love doesn't vanish, and neither does the legacy of those we've lost.

Journal Prompt:

How have the children in your family been affected by loss? What moments—conversations, questions, silences—have stayed with you? What do you wish you could say to comfort their hearts while still honoring your own?

_____

_____

_____

_____

_____

Affirmation:

I carry the stories that keep my loved ones alive. I honor their memory by loving the next generation with tenderness, truth, and hope.

Letter to Derrion – Dez's First Football Game

Dear Derry Don,

Your oldest son, Dez, played in his first football game recently.

I wish you could've seen him! I wish you could've stood on the sidelines with me, chest puffed up, cheering louder than anyone else. Because he's so much like you. The way he moves on the field. The fire in his eyes. The way he clutches that football like it belongs to him.

He loves the game just like you did—maybe even more. He plays football on the video game for hours—calling plays, trash-talking the screen, yelling like he's actually on the field. Just like you used to do. It's like he inherited your passion through his blood.

And it's not just talent—it's joy. He plays with a smile on his face every time he steps on that field. Other parents have even commented on it, how his joy is contagious, how it lights up the game. That's you, too. That infectious energy. That magnetic spirit.

He's a real competitor, fierce and focused. But he's also an encourager. A hype man for his teammates.

He plays with heart. With pride. With purpose. And every time I watch him, I feel you. I see you.

But I also miss you—deeply and painfully. I imagine you in the bleachers, shouting his name. Coaching him from the sidelines. Tossing the ball with him after practice. You would've been so proud. I can feel it. You live in him, Derrion. I see it more and more every day.

Not long ago, while he was visiting his mom, she texted me about how stubborn he was being. I just shook my head and said, *"He is a Robinson. Let's target and nurture his strengths and realign his weaknesses."* Because just like good genes are passed down, the tough ones can be too. But I believe in him. My goal is to cultivate the positive and redirect what needs refining.

And I'm doing my best to be there for him—your son. To love him the way I loved you. To remind him that he comes from someone fierce, passionate, gifted, and full of love.

You are still his father. And that will never change.

Love always,

Mama

Journal Prompt:

Think about a child in your life who reminds you of someone you've lost. What qualities do they carry that feel familiar or sacred? How do you want to nurture their gifts while also guiding their growth? Reflect on the legacy you're helping shape.

_____

_____

_____

_____

_____

Affirmation:

I honor the legacy of those I've loved by showing up with purpose, patience, and joy for the ones still growing under my care.

A Note I Can't Ignore

As much as I smile watching Dez on the field...

As much as I see Derrion in his stance, in his fire, in his joy...

I also carry something else.

The truth.

Derrion was still grappling with his addiction. Still struggling to be consistent. Still fighting demons he didn't always want to name. And as much as I believe in healing, I also know—if he hadn't found it—things between him and Dez might have been hard. Painful. Unpredictable.

I prayed for that healing. I still do.

Because as much as I wanted them to have time together, I also know what it's like to love someone who's not whole. And I wonder... would their relationship have been beautiful? Or would it have broken Dez the way it sometimes broke me?

That's a hard truth to sit with.

But I don't pretend here. I write what's real.

And the real truth is—I miss Derrion, and I also thank God that Dez can grow up with stability. With joy. With memories that are his. And I pray, every day, that what Derrion couldn't give, I can.

Because legacy isn't just about blood. It's about what we pass on.
And I want to pass on healing.

Journal Prompt:

What truths have you had to hold that are complicated, painful, or unfinished? How do you honor both the love and the reality of someone you've lost without editing their story?

_____

_____

_____

_____

_____

Affirmation:

It's okay to hold joy and truth at the same time. I honor my love by telling the whole story—not just the easy parts.

The MiMi Manifesto

A Note from MiMi

This isn't a farewell. It's a foundation.

I call it a manifesto, not because I'm done—but because I'm rooted. Rooted in love, in legacy, and in the life I'm still gratefully living. I plan to be around for a long time—taking GrandCations with your little hearts, traveling and exploring the world, being your biggest cheerleader for milestones and everyday accomplishments, and serving as a buffer of love in a sometimes cold world.

But I also know that words can outlive the moment. So I wrote this to be a guide. A reminder. A little bit of **MiMi**, in writing, for the days when you need a nudge, a memory, or just to feel close.

This is how I love. This is how I lead. This is how I hope you'll remember me—while I'm still here and even when I'm not.

— *MiMi*

To my grandchildren,

From a heart that holds both the weight of grief and the wonder of joy, this is what I want you to carry—with you now, and always:

- You are loved, completely and unconditionally, no matter what. No achievement, mistake or moment will ever change that.

- You are allowed to feel all your feelings—big or small, loud or quiet.

- Stay curious. Ask questions. Challenge what doesn't feel right. Use your voice.

- Family is more than blood. It's presence, consistency, and love. It's love you can count on, show up for, and grow with.

- Protect your peace fiercely, even if it means standing alone sometimes.

- Travel often. See the world. Make memories that make your soul smile.

- Laugh loud. Cry when you need to. Forgive, but don't forget the lessons.

- Your story matters—every chapter, even the hard ones.

- God is with you, even when it feels like silence.

- You come from strong people. You carry the resilience of those who came before you.

- You are already enough. You don't have to perform to be worthy. You were worthy from your very first breath.

- And whenever you wonder what MiMi would say, pause and listen. I've already whispered it into your spirit. I'm always in your heart, today and forever.

- Never forget: You are the legacy of a love that never dies.

You are my living legacy - Of love, of faith, and of grace

With Love In Every Season,
MiMi

Part VI: Legacy Letters

"What we leave behind isn't just memory—it's the love we speak out loud while we still can."
—Misty Reshun

When words go unspoken, they can either weigh us down or set us free. These are my letters—each one carrying truth, release, and remembrance. These letters are my way of speaking love out loud while I still can because legacy isn't what we leave behind. It's what we live into now.

- A Letter to My Younger Self
- A Letter to Derrion
- A Letter to the Women Who Loved Him
- A Note on Omission

A Letter to My Younger Self

Dear Me,

You're eighteen. You're pregnant. And you're scared.

You don't say it out loud, but I know what you're feeling—the swirl of emotions, the silence behind your eyes, the questions you can't quite shape into words yet. You are carrying a life inside of you—and the weight of a hundred unknowns.

You're already worrying about being a good mother. About how you'll finish school. About what people will think. You're hoping you won't let this child down. You're hoping you won't lose yourself.

There's so much you don't know yet.

You don't know how strong you are.
You don't know the ways your love will stretch, break, and rebuild.
You don't know that this child—this boy—will one day encourage you about having faith and tell you that *"Worrying is a sin,"* because he was paying attention in church at a young age.

And then, as years pass, he will be the source of your deepest worry.

He will battle demons you never saw coming.

And one day, he will break your heart into a million pieces as he raises his fist to you—something you never imagined, but something you will survive.

You'll carry grief in places you didn't know could ache. And just when you think you've cried your last tear, another wave will hit—unexpected and unforgiving.

Still, you'll breathe. You'll get up. You'll find purpose in the pieces.

Motherhood won't look the way you pictured. It won't be easy. But you will learn to love with a fierceness you didn't know existed. You will make mistakes. Big ones. But you will also keep showing up.

The child you carry? He will change your life. He will frustrate you, inspire you, challenge you. He will be your mirror and your mission. And one day, he will leave you. Far too soon. And you will grieve.

But even in that grief, you will still be a mother. And you will learn to hold joy and sorrow at the same time. You will find your voice. And you will use it to help others who are holding their own heartbreak.

You'll learn that setting boundaries isn't cruel—it's necessary. You'll stop over-explaining. You'll outgrow guilt. You'll realize that you can love someone deeply and still let go when your peace is on the line.

You will not be the same woman who started this journey. And that's okay.

She was brave, but you'll be wiser.

She was hopeful, but you'll be honest.

She dreamed of a perfect life. You'll build a real one.

So give yourself grace. Laugh louder. Rest more.

Tell the people you love how you feel while you still can.

And when life gets hard—when it threatens to break you—remember who you are. And whose you are.

I'm proud of you. I forgive you. I believe in you.

And one day, you'll understand just how sacred your journey really was.

With Love,

Me

Journal Prompt:

Write a letter to your younger self during a season of fear, change, or becoming. What did she/he need to hear? What do you know now that she/he couldn't have known then?

_____

_____

_____

_____

_____

Affirmation:

I honor the girl I was and the woman I've become. Every part of my journey matters—even the parts I didn't understand at the time.

A Letter to Derrion

Dear Derrion,

I was just a girl when I had you—barely old enough to understand what it meant to carry another life, let alone raise one. I gave you everything I had, and I know now that sometimes, what I had wasn't enough.

In my heart, I believed you never had to question whether I loved you. But the hard truth is, you did. You were the only child for eight years, and during that time, you may have grown used to love, attention, or material things coming easily. It gave you a sense of comfort, even entitlement when it came to being loved. And when your brother came along, that shift might have felt like a threat to everything you had known. I can see now how that could have been difficult, and I acknowledge it.

There were things you needed that I didn't always know how to give. I was just a young mother trying to figure it out—searching for love and a sense of belonging myself. Looking back, I can admit I was probably going about it all the wrong way.

And still, there are things I'll never understand. I'll never know what drove you to experiment with drugs—substances that changed you in ways I couldn't have imagined. I'll always wonder what you were trying to escape, or what you were searching for that you felt you couldn't find anywhere else. That question will stay with me for the rest of my life.

If I could sit with you now, I'd tell you this: I'm still learning. I'm still mothering you through memory, through legacy, through reflection. I did my best, baby. And I know my best may have hurt you. I forgive myself, even as I ache. And I pray you have forgiven me too.

I will always be your mama. I will always be reaching for you in the quiet. And I will always love you—through my flaws, through this grief, and far beyond this life.

Love always,

Mama

Journal Prompt:

What unanswered questions do you carry about your loved one's choices or struggles? Write them down without trying to solve or justify them. Then reflect on how you're learning to make peace with not knowing all the answers—and what love still looks like in that space of uncertainty.

_____

_____

_____

_____

_____

Affirmation:

Even in the silence of not knowing, I am still love in motion. My love is not diminished by my questions. I release the need for every answer, and I honor the love that endures beyond understanding.

A Letter To the Women Who Loved Him

There is a kind of pain that settles in a mother's soul when she learns that her son—her baby, her beloved—has caused harm. Not just to himself, but to others. Especially to women. Especially when I know that some of that harm was rooted in his own trauma, his own addiction, his own unraveling.

To the women who loved Derrion and endured manipulation, mistreatment, and/or abuse—please hear me: I am sorry.

As a woman, I see you. As a mother, I grieve with you. I imagine the confusion you must have felt, the hope you held onto, the moments of fear, the flickers of love that made you stay longer than you should have, or return when you needed to run.

I know that apologies do not erase scars. I know that my love for my son does not absolve the pain he caused. But I pray that naming it matters. I pray that this acknowledgment meets you with the dignity and grace you deserved all along.

I also want to say this—I know at times it appeared I did not like you. That was far from the truth. The truth is, I saw you as an enabler. One who was blinded by his dark eyebrows, magnetic smile, and confident swagger. He was a classic narcissist who preyed on those he could manipulate when it came to romantic relationships. It pained me to watch, and it broke something in me to know you were caught in the crossfire.

You were not crazy. You were not weak. You were not responsible for healing his wounds.

You were human. And you deserved tenderness, not turmoil.

I hope you are healing. I hope you are finding peace, finding your voice, finding safety.

And I hope that one day, the parts of you that got broken in loving him will rise up stronger and softer, sacred in the way only survivors know how to be.

With sorrow, with sisterhood, with sincerity—
A mother who sees you.

Journal Prompt:

What does accountability look like when love and harm are intertwined? Reflect on a time when someone you loved caused harm — to you or others. How did you reconcile the complexity of their actions with your own healing journey? What, if anything, still needs to be named or released?

_____

_____

_____

_____

_____

Affirmation:

I can grieve my child and still tell the truth. I choose compassion without denial, love without enabling and healing without pretending. My motherhood is still sacred.

A Note on Omission

If Derrion's behavior or addiction impacted you, and your story is not directly reflected in these pages, please know that the omission is not meant to minimize your experience.

Addiction leaves behind so many quiet ruptures, relationships frayed, hearts confused, and memories hard to speak aloud. In writing this book, I have tried to honor what I witnessed and what I held as a mother. But I also know there are others, friends, family, mentors, and peers, whose grief or pain may not be named here but is real and worthy just the same.

As I write these words, I am also learning to release the guilt, shame, and false responsibility I have carried for far too long. I am remorseful for the ways my son may have affected others, for the hurt he caused, knowingly or unknowingly. But I will not live in self-condemnation. I did the best I could with what I knew as a mother navigating love, fear, and brokenness. I am still learning. Still healing.

And the truth of the matter is, he was not all bad. He was layered, like most of us.

There may be some who read this book and cannot fathom or identify with the version of him I describe, because they experienced a different side of his story. I honor that, too. Both truths can exist at once.

If you have wonderful memories of him, cherish those and consider yourself blessed to carry the best parts of him in your memory and heart. Love does not have to be erased in order for pain to be acknowledged.

If your story was tangled with his in any way, if your healing has been slow or unspoken, I want you to know this: your pain matters. Your perspective is valid. And your healing journey deserves space, too.

Journal Prompt:

Think about someone in your life whose story is complex or unfinished in your heart. What parts of that story have gone unspoken, either by choice or by circumstance? What would it look like to honor your full truth without carrying guilt that does not belong to you?

Affirmation:

I release the weight of guilt that does not belong to me. Even unspoken pain deserves acknowledgment.

Part VII: What Remains

"Grief may shape us, but it does not get the final word. What remains is love, purpose, and the will to keep living with both."
—Misty Reshun

This final section is not an ending. It's a quiet reckoning with what endures — the lessons, the ache, the legacy, and the grace we give ourselves in the aftermath. These are the truths I carry forward, and maybe, the ones you will too.

Included Titles:

- Before the Spiral: What I Wish I'd Known Then
- The Weight We Carry
- In Lieu of Flowers: A Living Legacy
- The Things I Wish I Could Tell Him Now
- A Final Blessing

Before the Spiral: What I Wish I'd Known Then

I remember the moment I saw my Derrion smoking a cigarette.

He was in the 7th grade.

I had just left the house for work, passing him and his friends at the bus stop. But I forgot something and doubled back—and there he was, holding that cigarette like it belonged to him.

It broke something in me.

I lit into him right there on the sidewalk, full of anger, fear, and disappointment. Not just because of the cigarette, but because I knew what it could lead to.

First cigarettes, then marijuana, then God knows what else.

That moment didn't feel small. It felt like a warning. And even though I responded with rage, underneath it was a desperate kind of love—one that knew how quickly these "firsts" could snowball into something we'd never be able to take back.

Now let me be clear: I'm not saying that smoking always leads to something more sinister. Some kids experiment and walk away. But children at that age are not equipped to handle the responsibility of that choice—especially when addiction runs in the bloodline.

It's not just about the cigarette. It's about what it might awaken. About the doors, it might open before a child has the maturity to understand what's on the other side.

If you're a parent still in the thick of it, still fighting to keep your child from falling into the spiral of addiction, street life, or anything else that breaks the bond between who they are and who they were becoming—I want to talk to you.

I want to offer what I wish someone had offered me: not judgment, but guidance. Not fear, but tools. Not silence, but community.

What You Can Do Now

- Pay attention to the little things. That first cigarette matters. So does the change in tone, the new group of friends, the shift in eye contact. Small things often signal big storms.

- Stay calm, but stay present. I know how easy it is to respond with fury. But fear dressed as rage doesn't always reach them. Presence does. Let them know you see them—and you're not going anywhere.

- Ask real questions, and then listen. Not "what's wrong with you?" but "what's hurting you?" Not "Why would you do that?" but "What are you trying to escape?"

- Don't parent alone. Get help. Counseling, support groups, therapy—whatever it takes. This fight isn't meant to be fought solo. Release the shame.

- Separate shame from accountability. Hold them accountable, yes. But don't confuse accountability with shame. Shame shuts doors. Accountability opens the possibility of change.

- Reinforce the connection. Even when they push you away, remind them that the bond still exists. Keep saying "I love you," even if it goes unanswered. Those seeds still root.

And If You're Already in the Spiral...

Maybe the bond is already cracked. Maybe you're navigating addiction, estrangement, or daily survival. Maybe you're exhausted.

Let me say this:

It is not too late to love your child well.

It is not too late to get support.

It is not too late to forgive yourself.

It is not too late to choose boundaries without choosing abandonment.

It is not too late for healing, even if reconciliation never comes.

I despise the friend who gave Derrion his first cigarette. But the truth is, that friend was just the start. There was a whole world of pain waiting for him. And try as I might, I couldn't stop all of it.

But if this letter reaches even one parent standing at that same corner of early warning signs and heartbreak, then maybe it wasn't all in vain.

You still have time.

And even if you don't, you still have a voice. Use it. Tell your truth. Parent out loud. Love boldly.

Because silence never saved anyone.

Journal Prompt:

Think back to a moment when you noticed a shift in your child's behavior, energy, or choices. How did you respond in that moment—and how might you respond differently now, knowing what you know today?

If you are currently parenting a child through crisis or conflict, what support do you need to stay grounded and engaged?

Who can you invite into your corner so that you don't carry this alone?

_____

_____

_____

_____

_____

Affirmation:

I am not powerless. I can parent with presence, love, and truth—even in the hardest moments. I choose connection over control and hope over fear.

The Weight We Carry

Dear Mama, I See You

To every mother reading this, whether your arms are full or aching, your heart content or cracked wide open, I want you to know that I see you.

Motherhood is heavy. Not just the physical kind, the diaper bags, the midnight rocking, the sports schedules, but the emotional weight we carry that no one talks about. The kind that tucks itself between our ribs and settles in our throats when our children are hurting, lost, or simply different than we imagined.

Society has a strange way of celebrating us when our children shine, when they graduate, when they're polite, when they succeed, and shaming us when they stumble. If they struggle with addiction, get in trouble with the law, lash out, or drift away... somehow, we're seen as the failure. The thread that didn't hold.

But motherhood is not a formula. It's not "if you love hard enough, they'll turn out okay." It's not "pray and everything will be fine." It's messier than that. Holier than that. More human than that.

So to the mothers whose children walk a smooth road, I pray you walk it with humility. May you offer grace instead of judgment. Because not every mother got the same hand. Not every child came into the world with the same burdens or battles.

And to the mothers who are in the trenches, maybe watching a child spiral, or trying to love them from a distance, or carrying the grief of a future that won't be, I honor your fight. I honor your tears. I honor the choices you made with the information and energy you had at the time.

Sometimes there is no right decision, only the best one you can live with. You are not alone. You are not a bad mother. You are not a lost cause.

You are navigating a road with curves, potholes, and detours that others may never understand, but I do. I've walked it. I'm still walking it. And I want you to know: You are still worthy of love, community, and grace. Even when it's hard.
Especially when it's hard.

With you in the valley,
Misty

Journal Prompt:
Reflect on a time when you felt judged or misunderstood as a mother. What would you say to that version of yourself now — with more grace, wisdom, and compassion?

_____

_____

_____

_____

_____

Affirmation:
I release the shame that was never mine to carry. I am a mother doing her best in a world that doesn't always understand the weight I bear. I choose compassion over comparison, and grace over guilt.

In Lieu of Flowers: A Living Legacy

When Derrion passed, I didn't want flowers. I didn't want petals that would wilt or cards that would fade. I wanted purpose. I wanted impact. I wanted something that would live on.

So, in lieu of flowers, I asked for donations to *For Oak Cliff*, a nonprofit organization that had long been doing the work — building up our community, pouring into our youth, and turning pain into progress.

But I knew I wanted to do more.

Derrion was a writer. A thinker. A storyteller. His words held depth, even when his life was unraveling. He authored *The Love Boyz* and was working on a second book at the time of his death. So, to honor his creative spirit and his complex journey, I created The Derrion Robinson Literary Scholarship.

What began as a call for community support has now grown into something lasting — a scholarship housed within *The Derrion Robinson Literary Foundation*, created in his name and rooted in his love for storytelling.

The scholarship is awarded to high school graduates who are pursuing higher education — especially those with a passion for writing, literature, or storytelling in any form. It is my way of making sure that Derrion's story doesn't end with his last breath. It lives on in every student who picks up a pen, shares their truth, and chooses a different path.

This scholarship is not just about helping students pay for school. It's about honoring a life that was layered with both brilliance and brokenness. It's about creating something beautiful in the face of unimaginable grief. It's about turning mourning into momentum.

It is, in every way, *a living legacy*.

The Things I Wish I Could Tell Him Now

I talk to you in the quiet moments.

In the car, when a song plays that you used to love.

In the kitchen, when I catch myself making enough for one more

plate or fixing pork chops.

In the middle of the night, when the ache outpaces the hours.

I wish I could tell you that I understand more now.

That some of the things I used to say out of fear or frustration

were really just prayers disguised as rules.

That I know your pain wasn't always something you could name —

or explain.

But I saw it. I see it clearer now.

I wish I could tell you that Dez has your grin.

That sometimes when he laughs, it stops me in my tracks.

I wish you could see the way Za'Niyah is growing —

even though she was not your biological child,

I have taken on the responsibility of caring for her and her brother

Dez full-time.

She carries joy like a crown, and I know you'd be proud.

I wish I could tell you about the son you didn't get to meet —

Derrion Dante' Robinson Jr "Derry J".

He looks just like you.

There's something about his presence that feels like a continuation,

like the universe gave us another glimpse of you,

a piece of you that never had the chance to unfold beside you.

I tell them about you, but it's never enough.

How do I compress a whole life into a bedtime story?

I wish I could tell you that your book still sits on my shelf,

that I read your words when I need to hear your voice.

That your brilliance wasn't lost — it lingers.

And maybe one day, I'll help publish *Christian's Pain*

so the world knows what I already do:

you were a writer, a thinker, a truth-teller in progress.

I wish I could tell you I'm not angry anymore.

Not the way I was.

I've made peace with the mess, the love, the loss,

and the impossibly tangled lines between them.

I wish I could tell you I'm braver now.

Not because I wanted to be,

but because losing you forced me to be.

And maybe most of all,

I wish I could tell you

that even with the broken pieces,

you were always loved,

still are,

and always will be.

Journal Prompt:

What are the things left unsaid that still live inside you? If you could speak to your loved one now, what would you say — not to change the past, but to honor your present?

_____

_____

_____

_____

A Final Blessing

For every grieving parent, searching soul, and healing heart

May you walk gently with the weight you carry,

knowing it is not yours to bear alone.

May you forgive yourself for what you didn't know, for what you couldn't fix,

for the silence you filled with love the best way you knew how.

May you give yourself the grace you so freely offer others.

May you release the weight of perfection and rest in the truth that trying is enough.

May you remember that even the broken places can bloom, not despite the cracks, but because of them.

May you speak to yourself like someone you love, and may you love yourself like someone worth staying for.

May you find moments of peace that surprise you, and strength that doesn't shout, but steadies.

May your memories soften with time, and may your legacy — the one you're still building —

be shaped not only by what was lost, but by what remains.

May you no longer measure your healing in milestones or expectations, but in the quiet ways you choose to keep going, to keep loving, to keep breathing, even when it hurts.

If you are grieving, may peace visit you gently.

If you are parenting through pain, may strength rise within you.

If you are healing, may your healing come full and holy.

And when the silence is loud, may you hear the whisper: you are not alone. You are not alone in your sorrow. You are not broken beyond repair. You are not defined by what you could not save. You are still here. You are still worthy. You are still becoming.

And that is more than enough.

ABOUT THE AUTHOR

Misty Reshun is a mother, grandmother, and truth-teller whose life has been shaped by love, loss, and the fierce pursuit of healing. Born and raised in the Dallas/Fort Worth area, she holds a Master's degree in Human Rights and Social Justice. Her professional journey includes work as a Governance, Risk, and Compliance Manager, while her passion for advocacy and community organizing has been a consistent thread throughout her life.

She is the founder of the **Regal Sisterhood Book Club**, a nearly two-decade-old community rooted in sisterhood, storytelling, and sacred space for women who read, lead, and live with intention. An avid traveler turned part-time travel agent, Misty believes deeply in the power of experience, reflection, and storytelling to transform pain into purpose.

Sunflowers and Silence: Reflections from the Valley is her first book.

Contact Misty via email: MistyReshun@gmail.com

A Personal Note from the Author

I recently listened to Rickey Smiley talk about the complicated grief he carries after losing his son, Brandon. He said, *"I didn't get to say goodbye. And I didn't get a chance to fix it."* That line hit me hard. When Derrion passed I had not spoken to him in over 365 days. With our last encounter, I drew a hard line in the sand. Like Rickey, I couldn't ignore the disrespect.

Grief is heavy enough when someone we love dies. But when the relationship was strained, or filled with worry, silence, or pain, it brings another layer entirely.

Some of us are grieving people we couldn't save.

Some of us are grieving relationships that ended before healing could happen.

Some of us are still here, holding on to hope... or trying to let go.

This book, and the pen-to-paper process behind it, began in that moment. I write for anyone who has loved deeply, lost painfully, or struggled to make peace with a complicated goodbye.

If you've had to set boundaries with someone you love...

If you've worried yourself sick...

If you've had to protect your peace while still caring deeply...

If you never got to say goodbye...

If you've ever loved someone who struggled...

If you've ever had to choose distance over dysfunction…

If you're trying to make peace with a complicated story…

I see you.

You are not alone.

I wrote this for us.

With love and understanding,

Misty Reshun

Legacy in Action:

The Derrion Robinson Literary Foundation

The **Derrion Robinson Literary Foundation** was created to honor the life, voice, and creative brilliance of **Derrion Dante' Robinson** — a young Black writer, son, father, and dreamer whose story continues through others.

Through the foundation's flagship initiative, **The Derrion Robinson Literary Scholarship**, we award scholarships to graduating high school seniors pursuing higher education and having a passion for writing, storytelling, or literature. This is one small way we ensure Derrion's name lives on — in purpose, not just in memory.

If you would like to learn more or support the foundation's mission, please contact:
derrionrobinsonfoundation@gmail.com

Because stories deserve to rise.
Because his legacy still has chapters left to write.

Resources for Grieving and Struggling Parents

Whether you're grieving the loss of a child, navigating a strained relationship, or healing from years of silence, please know: you are not alone. The following organizations, books, and digital spaces have supported countless parents through sorrow, conflict, and the complexity of love that doesn't always fit clean lines. May these resources guide your steps forward — even the trembling ones.

Organizations & Support Networks

- The Compassionate Friends – Grief support after the death of a child:
  www.compassionatefriends.org

- GriefShare – Local and online grief support groups:
  www.griefshare.org

- SADOD (Support After Death by Overdose) – Resources for overdose-related grief:
  www.sadod.org

- National Alliance for Children's Grief – Support for families and professionals:
  www.childrengrieve.org

- Partnership to End Addiction – Resources for families struggling with a loved one's substance use:
  www.drugfree.org

- PAL (Parents of Addicted Loved Ones) – Faith-based support group for parents:
  www.palgroup.org

- Not My Son – A community organization committed to preventing gun violence and supporting families affected by it. They offer advocacy, education, and support services to empower communities and honor the lives lost.
  www.notmyson.org

Books to Hold Your Heart

- *It's OK That You're Not OK* by Megan Devine

- *Bearing the Unbearable* by Joanne Cacciatore

- *The Grieving Parent's Book of Hope* by Norma Sawyers-Kurz

- *The Deepest Well* by Dr. Nadine Burke Harris

- *Loving Someone with Addiction* by Candace Plattor

- *Setting Boundaries with Your Adult Children* by Allison Bottke

- *Parents Who Hurt* by Paul Hegstrom

Podcasts & Digital Spaces

- Terrible, Thanks for Asking (Nora McInerny) – Honest storytelling around grief and loss

- The Leftover Pieces – For suicide loss survivors

- What's Your Grief? – Practical tools and emotional support

- Beyond Addiction – CRAFT model for families navigating substance use

- Instagram:

  - @refugeingrief

  - @griefcoach

  - @modernloss

  - @therapyforblackgirls

You don't have to have all the answers. You just have to keep breathing. And when you're ready — reach. Heal. Reconnect. Release. Whatever the next step looks like for you, may it be held with grace.

www.ingramcontent.com/pod-product-compliance
Lightning Source LLC
Chambersburg PA
CBHW021633120626
46545CB00002B/519